Planets

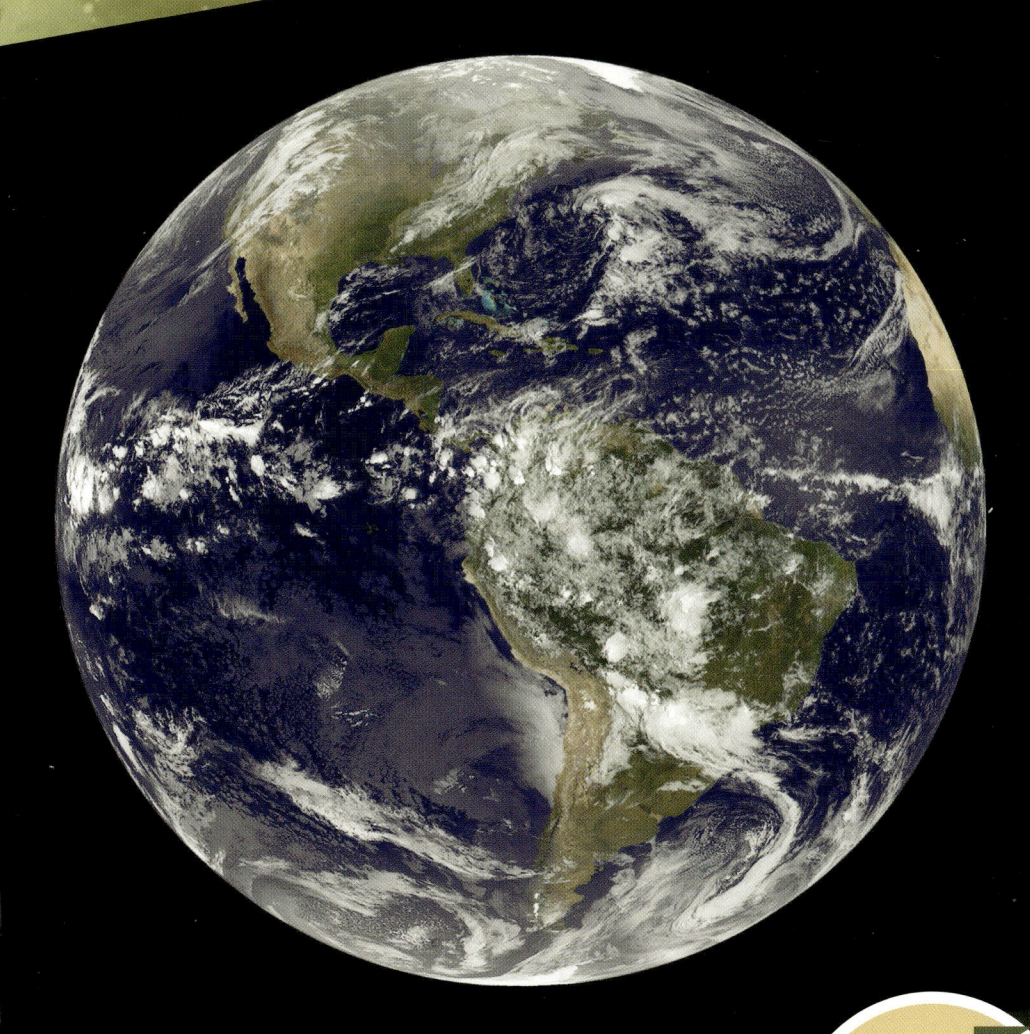

Earth

Dash!
LEVELED READERS
An Imprint of Abdo Zoom • abdobooks.com

3

Dash!
LEVELED READERS

Level 1 – Beginning
Short and simple sentences with familiar words or patterns for children who are beginning to understand how letters and sounds go together.

Level 2 – Emerging
Longer words and sentences with more complex language patterns for readers who are practicing common words and letter sounds.

Level 3 – Transitional
More developed language and vocabulary for readers who are becoming more independent.

abdobooks.com

Published by Abdo Zoom, a division of ABDO, PO Box 398166, Minneapolis, Minnesota 55439. Copyright © 2019 by Abdo Consulting Group, Inc. International copyrights reserved in all countries. No part of this book may be reproduced in any form without written permission from the publisher. Dash!™ is a trademark and logo of Abdo Zoom.

Printed in the United States of America, North Mankato, Minnesota.
092018
012019

Photo Credits: Getty Images, iStock, NASA, Shutterstock
Production Contributors: Kenny Abdo, Jennie Forsberg, Grace Hansen, John Hansen
Design Contributors: Dorothy Toth, Neil Klinepier

Library of Congress Control Number: 2018946215

Publisher's Cataloging in Publication Data

Names: Murray, Julie, author.
Title: Earth / by Julie Murray.
Description: Minneapolis, Minnesota : Abdo Zoom, 2019 | Series: Planets |
    Includes online resources and index.
Identifiers: ISBN 9781532125263 (lib. bdg.) | ISBN 9781641856713 (pbk) |
    ISBN 9781532126284 (ebook) | ISBN 9781532126796 (Read-to-me ebook)
Subjects: LCSH: Earth (Planet)--Juvenile literature. | Earth (Planet)--Miscellanea--
    Juvenile literature. | Planets--Juvenile literature. | Solar system--Juvenile literature.
Classification: DDC 550--dc23

THIS BOOK CONTAINS RECYCLED MATERIALS

Table of Contents

Earth 4

Inside Earth 12

On the Surface 14

More Facts 22

Glossary 23

Index 24

Online Resources 24

Earth

Sun

Mercury

Earth

Venus

4

Earth is the fifth-biggest planet in our **solar system**. It is the third planet from the sun. It has one moon. Earth is also our home!

6

Earth's **atmosphere** is made up of gases that living things need to survive, like oxygen. It protects the planet. It also helps manage Earth's temperature, which is 59 °F (15 °C) on average.

8

Earth orbits the sun. It takes 365 days to go one time around. It also spins, or rotates, as it orbits. Earth completes one rotation every 24 hours. This gives us day and night.

Earth is tilted on its **axis**. This creates the seasons. When the Northern Hemisphere is tilted toward the sun, it is summer there and winter in the Southern Hemisphere. Six months later, the seasons are the opposite.

Summer

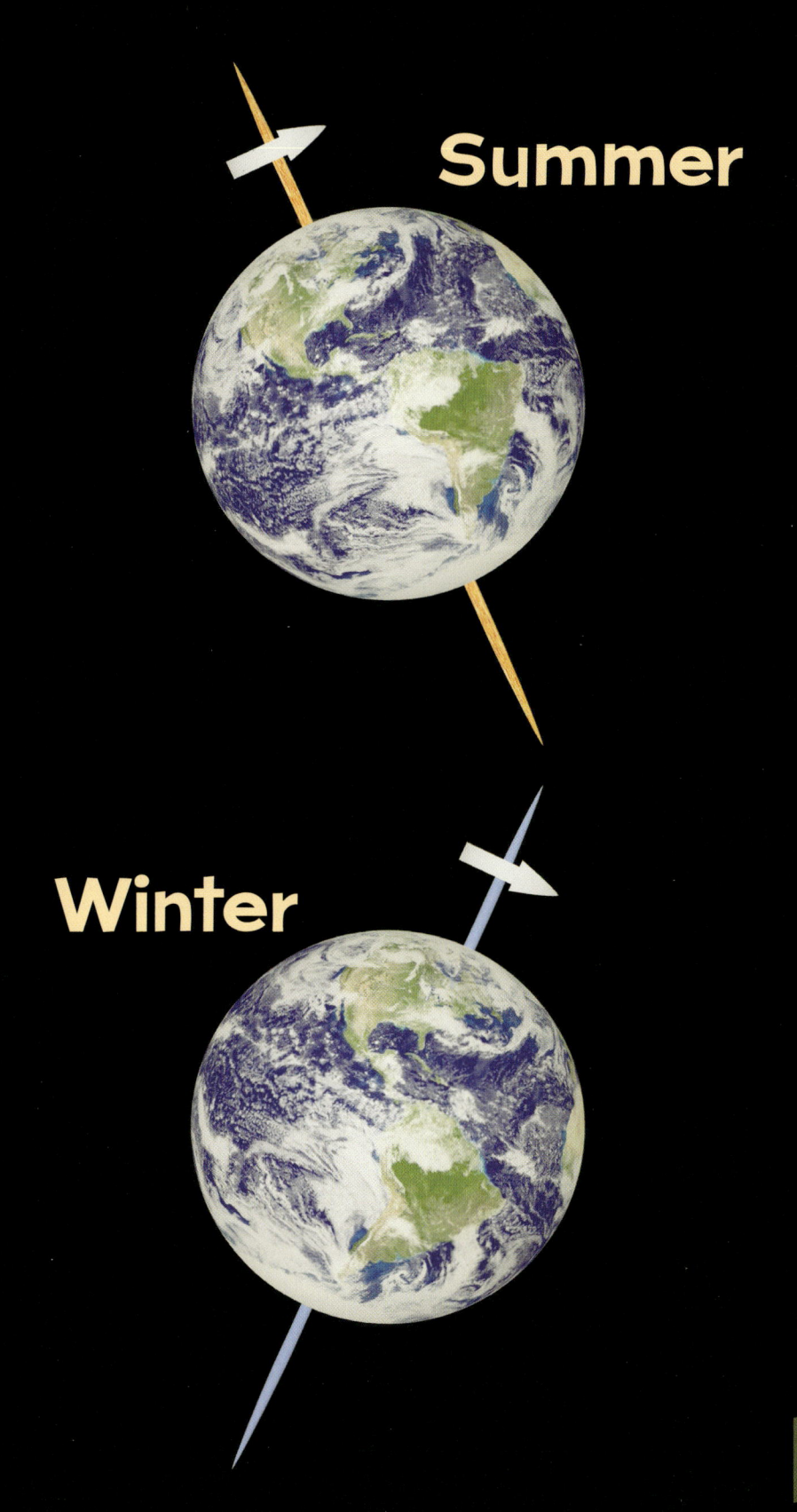

Winter

11

Inside Earth

Earth is mainly made up of rock. It has many layers. The center is a solid core. The outer core is made up of a hot liquid. The mantle makes up 84% of Earth's volume. The crust is the thin outside layer of rock. We live on the crust!

Inner Core

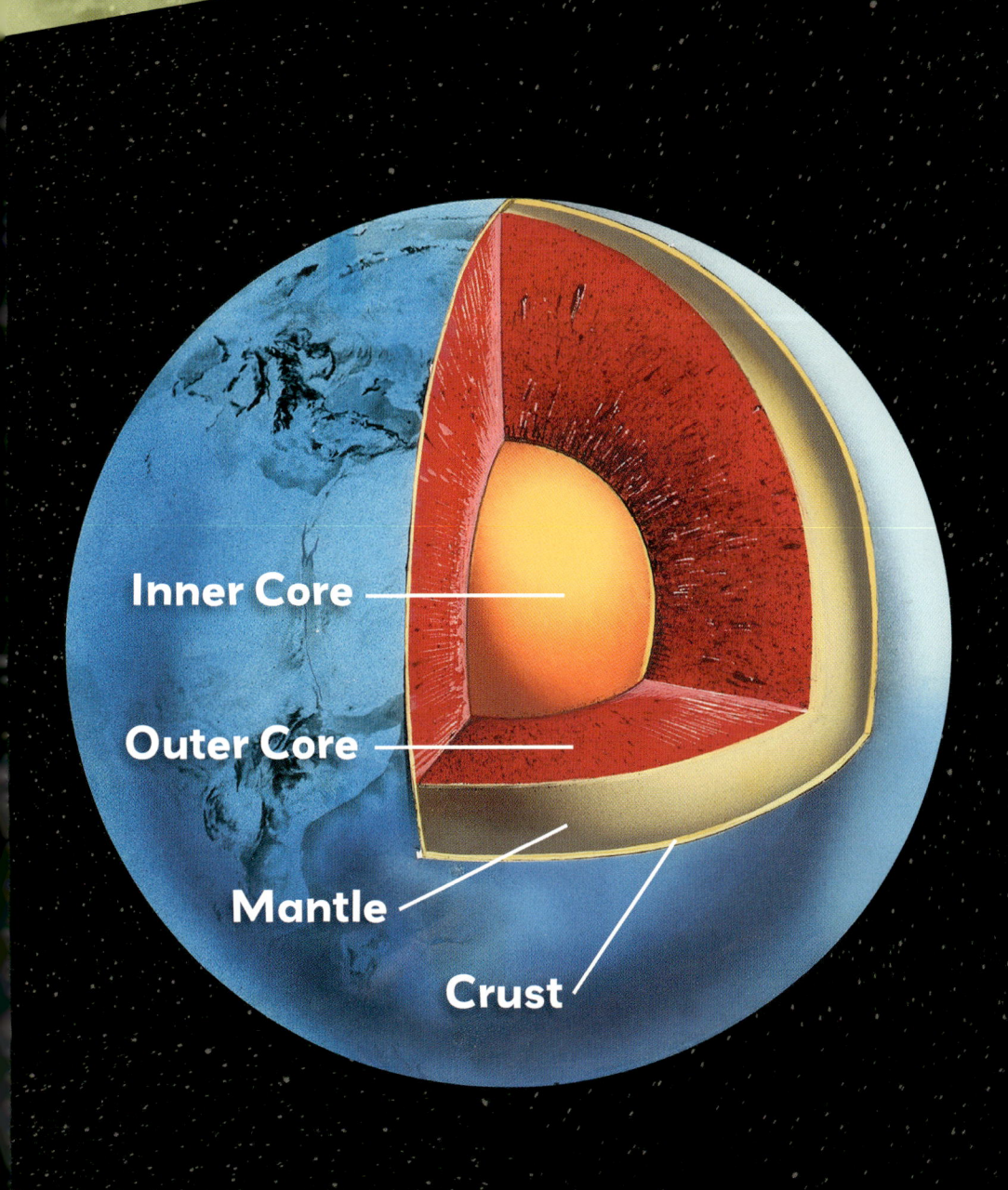

Outer Core

Mantle

Crust

13

On the Surface

About 70% of Earth's surface is covered in water. Water can be found in the form of a solid, liquid, or gas.

The Pacific Ocean is the largest body of water. It holds more than half of Earth's liquid water. Fresh water makes up only 2.5% of water on Earth.

Many different kinds of plants and animals live in both salt and fresh water.

18

Land makes up about 30% of Earth's surface. Billions of humans, animals, insects, and plants live on land.

North America

Europe

Asia

Africa

South America

Australia

Antarctica

20

Earth has 7 **continents**. Each continent is **dynamic** and beautiful. There are mountains, canyons, deserts, and plains to be seen all around Earth!

More Facts

- Scientists believe that Earth is about 4.5 billions years old.

- It takes more than 8 minutes for sunlight to reach Earth. This is because the sun is 93 million miles (149.7 million km) away!

- Earth moves 67,000 miles per hour (107,826 km/h) through space. That is 18.5 miles (29.7 km) per second!

Glossary

atmosphere – the gases surrounding the earth or other planets in our solar system.

axis – an imaginary line about which an object turns.

continent – one of the earth's seven major areas of land.

dynamic – always active and changing.

solar system – a system that includes a star (the sun) and all of the matter which orbits it, including planets and their moons.

Index

atmosphere 7

core 12

crust 12

day 9

land 19, 21

life 7, 17, 19

mantle 12

moon 5

seasons 10

size 5

sun 5, 9

temperature 7

water 15, 16, 17

year 9

Online Resources

Booklinks NONFICTION NETWORK
FREE! ONLINE NONFICTION RESOURCES

To learn more about Earth, please visit **abdobooklinks.com**. These links are routinely monitored and updated to provide the most current information available.